Visitors to Bayon
Temple in Cambodia
travel by elephant.

A monastery sits on the island Mont Saint-Michel off the coast of France.

LITTLE KIDS
FIRST
BIG
BOOK OF THE
WORLD

ELIZABETH CARNEY

NATIONAL
GEOGRAPHIC
KiDS

WASHINGTON, D.C.

CONTENTS

INTRODUCTION

Would you like to learn about the whole world without leaving this very spot? You can with this atlas! An atlas is a book of maps. What is a map anyway? It's a drawing of a place as it looks from above. This book has maps of the world's continents. You'll see the shapes, locations, and features of Earth's seven major landmasses. On pages 8 and 9, you will see examples of maps that show the land and places on Earth. An atlas usually gives you more information than just maps. In this book, you'll find out about each continent's countries, land and weather, people, animals, and major sights.

NATIONAL GEOGRAPHIC'S *LITTLE KIDS FIRST BIG BOOK OF THE WORLD* IS ORGANIZED BY CONTINENT, FEATURING EVERYTHING A YOUNG EXPLORER NEEDS TO LEARN THE LAY OF THE LAND:

COUNTRIES

Discover maps that present the countries of our world and learn which nations are considered the largest and smallest of their continent.

LAND AND WEATHER

Discover a variety of landscapes with land maps that illustrate each continent's peaks and valleys, waterways and grasslands, and learn about the different types of weather and seasons around the globe.

PEOPLE

Learn about the diverse groups of people who live on each continent. Find out where they came from and how they got there.

ANIMALS

Discover some of the most interesting animals that live on each continent and find out where they make their homes, what they eat, and more.

SIGHTS

Uncover the world's most fascinating sights and the history behind their famous existence.

EXPLORER SPOTLIGHTS

Meet some amazing explorers on missions of discovery around the world and see what they have found.

HOW TO USE THIS BOOK

FACT BOXES give a quick look at important information about a continent. How many countries does it have? Which one is the smallest? Which is the biggest? Which city has the most people? You'll find the answers in the fact boxes.

POP-UP FACTS offer tidbits of really cool information. Use these to impress your friends and family with your geo knowledge.

THE COUNTRIES
An icy north and a tropical south

You'll find palm trees and sunshine on the Caribbean islands. The United States, Canada, and Mexico make up most of North America.

The land between Mexico and South America is often called Central America.

Where is the world's largest island? It's icy Greenland to the northeast of Canada.

A MALE ELK IN CANADA

Can you see how this continent is shaped like a triangle?

12

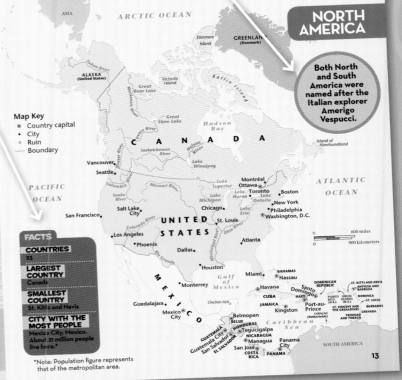

NORTH AMERICA

Both North and South America were named after the Italian explorer Amerigo Vespucci.

Map Key
⊛ Country capital
• City
⋏ Ruin
······ Boundary

FACTS

COUNTRIES
23

LARGEST COUNTRY
Canada

SMALLEST COUNTRY
St. Kitts and Nevis

CITY WITH THE MOST PEOPLE
Mexico City, Mexico. About 21 million people live here.*

*Note: Population figure represents that of the metropolitan area.

13

QUESTIONS relate the information back to you and your life. They can even start a conversation.

LET'S GO! At the end of each section you'll find activities to try, each involving art, science, math, writing, or a physical activity.

PARENT TIPS in the back of this book provide games, activities, and project ideas. Parents can use these tips to help kids make more geography connections. There's also a glossary, a list of words and their meanings.

MAP OF THE WORLD

MAPS tell you what a place is like, even if you've never been there. Maps can also help you get where you want to go. They often use drawings called **symbols** to show things. A **map key** tells you what those symbols mean.

For example, a black solid line means the boundary between countries. A black dot stands for a city. If you don't know what a symbol on a map means, check the map key.

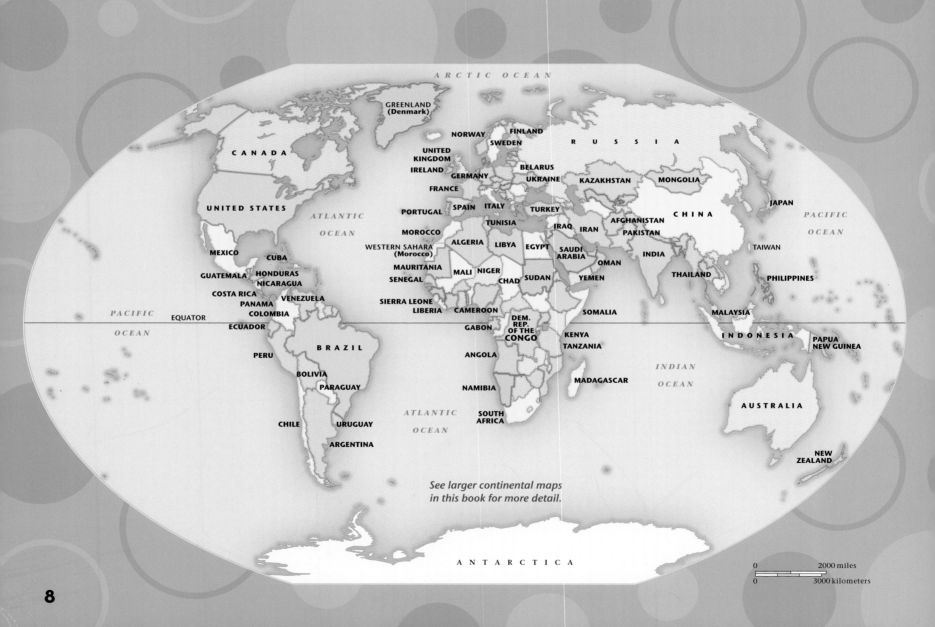

See larger continental maps in this book for more detail.

8

There are two main types of maps. **Political maps** show the outlines of countries. They can also mark the location of cities and capitals. **Physical maps** are the second type of map. These maps show an area's land and water features. You can see the locations of mountain ranges, forests, deserts, plains, and bodies of water such as lakes, rivers, and oceans.

Map Key

Mountain   Arid (Dry area)   Coniferous forest   Deciduous forest   Rain forest   Grassland   Wetland   Tundra   Ice cap

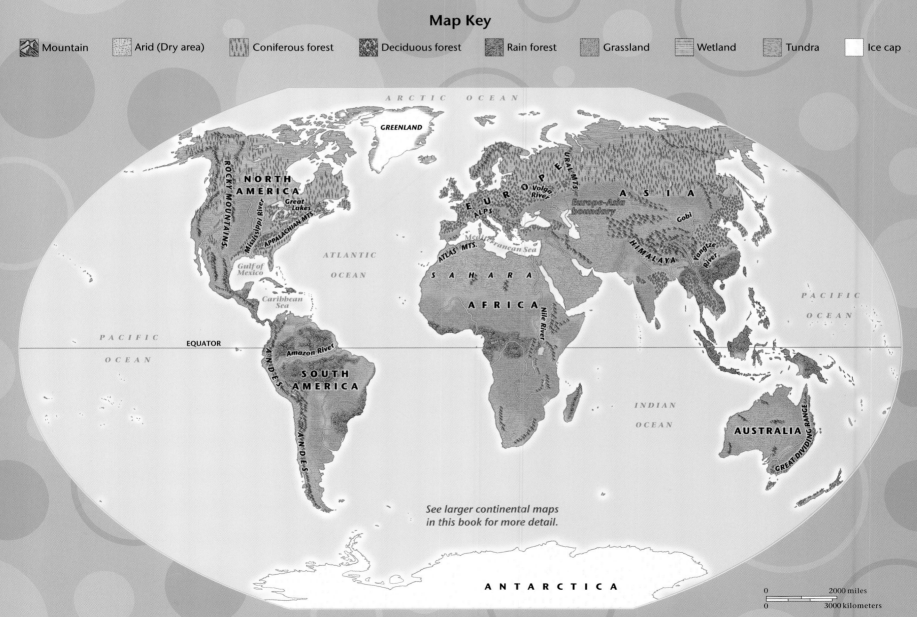

See larger continental maps in this book for more detail.

0   2000 miles

0   3000 kilometers

CHAPTER 1

NORTH AMERICA

A BISON HERD IN ALBERTA, CANADA

Land of many landscapes

THE COUNTRIES

An icy north and a tropical south

You'll find palm trees and sunshine on the Caribbean islands. The United States, Canada, and Mexico make up most of North America.

The land between Mexico and South America is often called Central America.

Where is the world's largest island? It's icy Greenland to the northeast of Canada.

A MALE ELK IN CANADA

Can you see how this continent is shaped like a triangle?

NORTH AMERICA

Both North and South America were named after the Italian explorer Amerigo Vespucci.

Map Key
- ⊛ Country capital
- • City
- ∴ Ruin
- ..... Boundary

*Note: Population figure represents that of the metropolitan area.

ARCTIC OCEAN

ASIA

Ellesmere Island

GREENLAND (Denmark)

ALASKA (United States)

Yukon River

Victoria Island

Baffin Island

Great Bear Lake

Mackenzie River

Great Slave Lake

Peace River

Hudson Bay

Island of Newfoundland

C A N A D A

Saskatchewan River

Nelson River

Lake Winnipeg

Fraser River

Vancouver

Seattle

Columbia River

Lake Superior

Montréal
Ottawa ⊛

Toronto

Boston

PACIFIC OCEAN

Snake River

Missouri River

Lake Michigan

Lake Huron

Lake Ontario

Lake Erie

New York

ATLANTIC OCEAN

San Francisco

Salt Lake City

Chicago

St. Louis

Philadelphia
⊛ Washington, D.C.

Los Angeles

Colorado River

U N I T E D S T A T E S

Ohio River

Mississippi River

Phoenix

Dallas

Atlanta

0   600 miles
0   900 kilometers

Rio Grande

Houston

M E X I C O

Monterrey

Miami

Gulf of Mexico

BAHAMAS
⊛ Nassau

Guadalajara

Mexico City ⊛

Chichén Itzá ∴

⊛ Havana

CUBA

Santo Domingo

DOMINICAN REPUBLIC

ST. KITTS AND NEVIS

ANTIGUA AND BARBUDA

HAITI

PUERTO RICO (U.S.)

VIRGIN ISLANDS (U.S.)

DOMINICA

ST. LUCIA

JAMAICA

Kingston

Port-au-Prince

CURAÇAO (Netherlands)

ST. VINCENT AND THE GRENADINES

BARBADOS

GRENADA

TRINIDAD AND TOBAGO

Belmopan
BELIZE

Caribbean Sea

GUATEMALA
Guatemala City ⊛

HONDURAS

Tegucigalpa

San Salvador ⊛
EL SALVADOR

NICARAGUA

⊛ Managua

Panama City ⊛

San José ⊛
COSTA RICA

PANAMA

SOUTH AMERICA

THE **LAND**

Near the North Pole, the land and ocean are often frozen. The flat land in the central plains is great for farming.

KULUSUK, GREENLAND

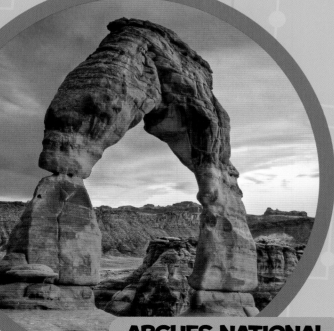

ARCHES NATIONAL PARK, UTAH, U.S.A.

In the southwest, you'll find deserts and rocky canyons. Steamy jungles grow in the southern part of the continent.

This type of cactus can live up to 200 years!

SAGUARO CACTUS IN ARIZONA, U.S.A.

NORTH AMERICA

(Denali) Mt. McKinley (6,194 m) 20,320 ft
Highest elevation in North America

Death Valley (-86 m) -282 ft
Lowest elevation in North America

ASIA

ARCTIC OCEAN

GREENLAND

PACIFIC OCEAN

Brooks Range
Yukon River
Mackenzie River
Great Bear Lake
Great Slave Lake
Hudson Bay
ROCKY MOUNTAINS
GREAT PLAINS
Columbia River
Sierra Nevada
Colorado River
Lake Winnipeg
Missouri River
Great Lakes
Mississippi River
Ohio River
APPALACHIAN MOUNTAINS
ATLANTIC OCEAN
Rio Grande
SIERRA MADRE OCCIDENTAL
SIERRA MADRE ORIENTAL
Gulf of Mexico
WEST INDIES
Caribbean Sea
CENTRAL AMERICA
SOUTH AMERICA

Map Key
- Mountain
- Arid (Dry area)
- Coniferous forest
- Deciduous forest
- Rain forest
- Grassland
- Wetland
- Tundra
- Ice cap

FACTS

SIZE
9,449,000 square miles
(24,474,000 sq km)

HIGHEST MOUNTAIN
Mount McKinley
(Denali), Alaska, U.S.A.

LOWEST PLACE
Death Valley,
California, U.S.A.

LONGEST RIVER
Mississippi River, U.S.A.

LARGEST LAKE
Lake Superior, U.S.A.
and Canada

0   600 miles
0   900 kilometers

15

More tornadoes form in the United States than anywhere else on Earth.

A BEACH IN TULUM, MEXICO

THE WEATHER

Hot in the south, chilly in the north

In the south, it's warm year-round, and many days are sunny!

Farther north, seasons bring cool autumn weather and rainy springs. It's cold all the time in the northernmost part of the continent. The ground is always frozen.

THE PEOPLE

People from all over the world have moved here.

GIRLS IN GUATEMALA

More than 8,000 years ago, people from Asia made their way across a land bridge to North America. More recently, people from all over the world have settled here. That's why North America has many different cultures.

People celebrate where they're from with parades, festivals, and sporting events.

Basketball was invented in North America in 1891.

A BASKETBALL GAME IN PENNSYLVANIA, U.S.A.

Kids go tobogganing (a type of sledding) in Nunavut, Canada's northernmost territory.

NUNAVUT, CANADA

MOTHER AND BABY POLAR BEARS

Manatees have fingernails on their front flippers.

THE ANIMALS

From musk oxen to manatees

Many types of animals live in North America. Some, like musk oxen and polar bears, are built for the cold. You can find manatees in waters of the warm south.

MUSK OX

SQUIRREL MONKEY

MILITARY MACAW

Parrots and monkeys squawk and screech in the rain forests of Central America.

21

THE **SIGHTS**

Old stone pyramids and a monumental gift

North America has many natural wonders, like the Grand Canyon. There are man-made ones, too.

GRAND CANYON, U.S.A.

CHICHÉN ITZÁ, MEXICO

The Maya people of Mexico and northern Central America built great stone pyramids long ago. These pyramids still stand today.

The Statue of Liberty stands in New York Harbor. France gave it to the United States as a gift.

The Statue of Liberty stands 305 feet (93 m) tall.

A symbol most people aren't able to see: Lady Liberty has a broken chain wrapped around her feet. It stands for the freedom that people find in the United States.

LET'S GO!

Sing in three languages

Most North Americans speak Spanish, English, or French. Try singing "Frère Jacques" in the three primary languages of North America.

Fray Felipe
(Spanish)

Fray Felipe, Fray Felipe,
¿Duermes tú? ¿Duermes tú?
¡Suenan las campanas!
¡Suenan las campanas!
Ding, dang, dong. Ding, dang, dong.

Frère Jacques
(French)

Frère Jacques, Frère Jacques,
Dormez-vous? Dormez-vous?
Sonnez les matines! Sonnez les matines!
Ding, dang, dong. Ding, dang, dong.

Brother John
(English)

Are you sleeping, are you sleeping,
Brother John? Brother John?
Morning bells are ringing!
Morning bells are ringing!
Ding, dang, dong.
Ding, dang, dong.

This continent is home to the world's largest rain forest and its driest desert.

THE COUNTRIES

From big Brazil to small Suriname

South America has 12 countries. Farming is important here.

Many foods come from this continent. Potatoes, tomatoes, and bananas are a few.

Most big cities are near the coasts.

A BEACH IN RIO DE JANEIRO, BRAZIL

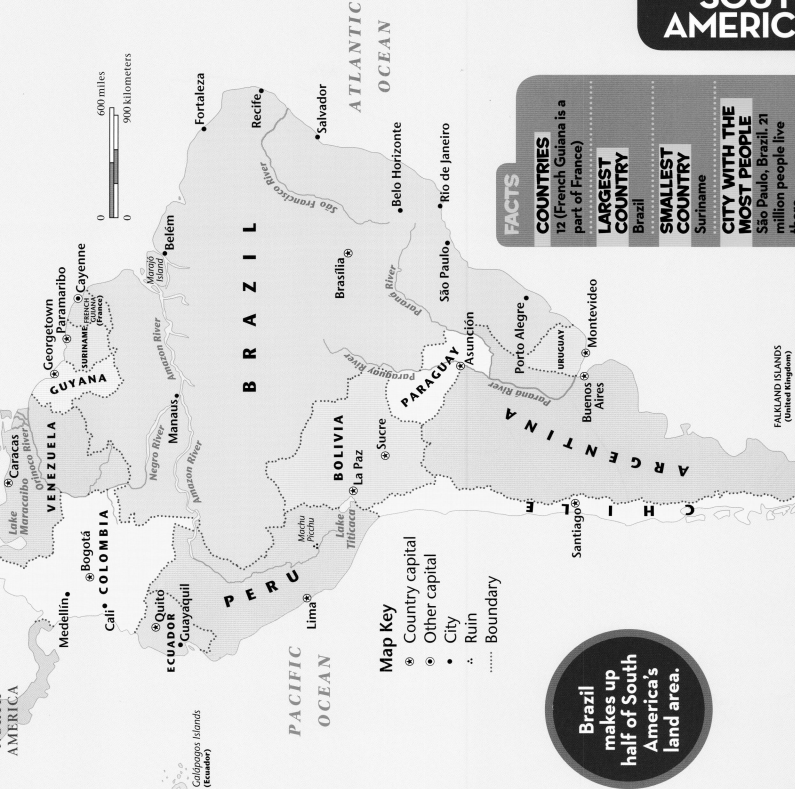

SOUTH AMERICA

ATLANTIC OCEAN

Fortaleza

Recife

Salvador

São Francisco River

Belo Horizonte

Rio de Janeiro

Belém

Brasília

São Paulo

Marajó Island

Cayenne
FRENCH GUIANA (France)

Georgetown
Paramaribo
SURINAME

Paraná River

Porto Alegre

Amazon River

GUYANA

Negro River

Asunción

Montevideo

URUGUAY

Manaus

B R A Z I L

PARAGUAY

Paraguay River

Buenos Aires

Caracas
Orinoco River

VENEZUELA

Paraná River

SOUTH GEORGIA (United Kingdom)

Lake Maracaibo

Amazon River

BOLIVIA

Sucre

La Paz

A R G E N T I N A

FALKLAND ISLANDS (United Kingdom)

Stanley

Bogotá

COLOMBIA

Machu Picchu

Lake Titicaca

C H I L E

Medellín

Cali

Quito

ECUADOR
Guayaquil

P E R U

Lima

Santiago

Map Key
- ⊛ Country capital
- ◉ Other capital
- • City
- ∴ Ruin
- ⋯⋯ Boundary

Galápagos Islands (Ecuador)

PACIFIC OCEAN

NORTH AMERICA

Brazil makes up half of South America's land area.

600 miles
900 kilometers
0
0

29

THE LAND

The world's longest mountain range and its second longest river are here.

The Andes mountain range stretches down the west side of South America. Some of these mountains are volcanoes!

The Amazon River is very long. It snakes through the Amazon rain forest.

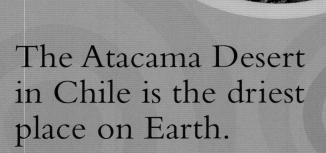

AMAZON RIVER

Parts of the Atacama Desert haven't seen a drop of rain since people began keeping weather records 400 years ago!

LOS FLAMENCOS NATIONAL RESERVE, CHILE

The Atacama Desert in Chile is the driest place on Earth.

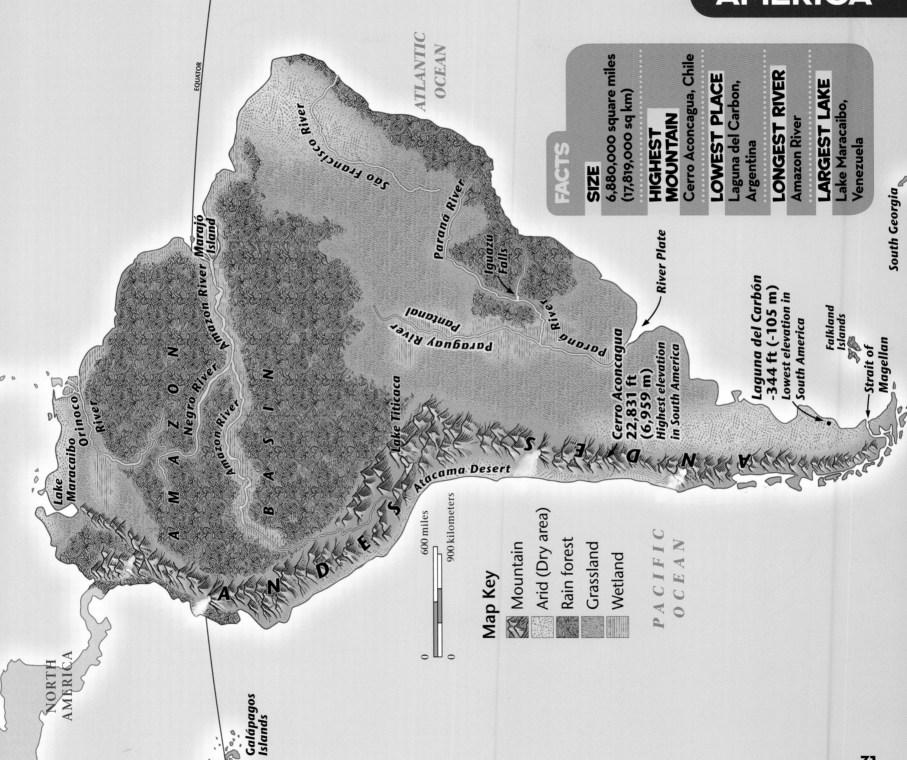

SOUTH AMERICA

FACTS

SIZE
6,880,000 square miles
(17,819,000 sq km)

HIGHEST MOUNTAIN
Cerro Aconcagua, Chile

LOWEST PLACE
Laguna del Carbon, Argentina

LONGEST RIVER
Amazon River

LARGEST LAKE
Lake Maracaibo, Venezuela

ATLANTIC OCEAN

EQUATOR

São Francisco River

Paraná River

Iguazú Falls

River Plate

Paraná River

Paraguay River

Pantanal

Marajó Island

Amazon River

Negro River

Amazon River

A M A Z O N   B A S I N

Orinoco River

Lake Maracaibo

NORTH AMERICA

Galápagos Islands

Amazon River

Lake Titicaca

Atacama Desert

A N D E S

Cerro Aconcagua
22,831 ft
(6,959 m)
Highest elevation in South America

Laguna del Carbón
-344 ft (-105 m)
Lowest elevation in South America

Falkland Islands

Strait of Magellan

South Georgia

PACIFIC OCEAN

600 miles
900 kilometers
0
0

Map Key
Mountain
Arid (Dry area)
Rain forest
Grassland
Wetland

The ice fields at Glaciers National Park in Argentina are the largest outside of Antarctica.

GLACIERS NATIONAL PARK, PATAGONIA, ARGENTINA

THE WEATHER

Rain forest bound? Bring your umbrella!

It's hot and rainy in the northern half of South America. The Amazon rain forest is here. Parts of the forest get up to nine feet (2.7 m) of rain a year.

The southern tip of South America is very cold. That's because it's so far away from the Equator. Giant ice sheets cover some parts of the land there.

TUMUCUMAQUE NATIONAL PARK, BRAZIL

The Amazon rain forest is the largest tropical rain forest in the world.

THE PEOPLE

Olá! Hola! That's how most people say "hello" in South America.

PERUVIAN GIRL

Very long ago, people made their way from Asia across North America into South America. Over time, they built great cities. People from Europe and Africa came later.

WHITE-WATER RAFTERS IN ECUADOR

Today, most South Americans are related to Asian, European, or African groups. Portuguese and Spanish are the main languages.

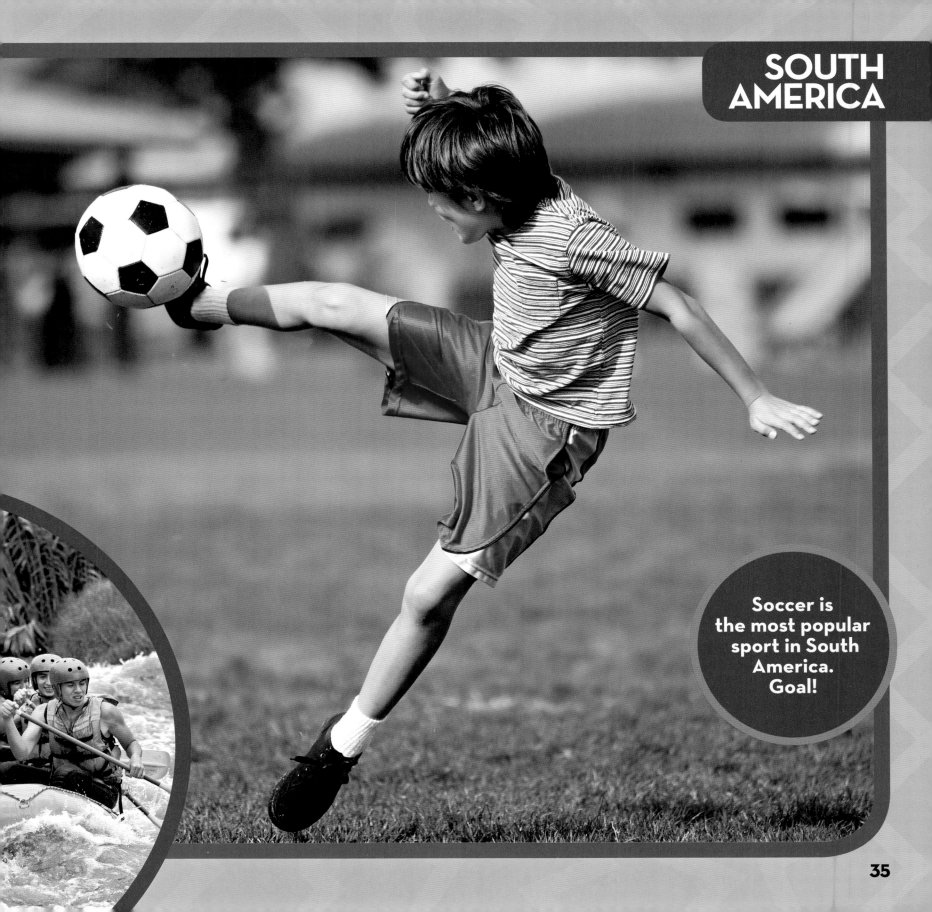

Soccer is the most popular sport in South America. Goal!

35

Guanacos are related to camels. They live on the plains, plateaus, and coastlines of Peru, Chile, and Argentina. They also live in the Andes.

ARMADILLO

A type of parrot, the blue-and-yellow macaw has a powerful beak for cracking nuts and seeds.

THE ANIMALS

Critters in a rainbow of colors

A wide variety of animals live in South America. There are blue-and-yellow macaws, poison dart frogs, and pink river dolphins in the rain forest.

POISON
DART FROG

PINK RIVER
DOLPHIN

You'll find llamas in the mountains. Armadillos live in different areas of the continent.

37

THE SIGHTS
Hiking boots and dancing shoes

Travelers hike a long way to see stone ruins on a mountaintop in Peru. The site is called Machu Picchu. It's known as the Lost City of the Inca. The Inca were ancient South American people.

A CARNIVAL FESTIVAL

Many South Americans celebrate Carnival. It's a festive season, usually in February. In Rio de Janeiro, Brazil, people wear colorful costumes and dance in the streets.

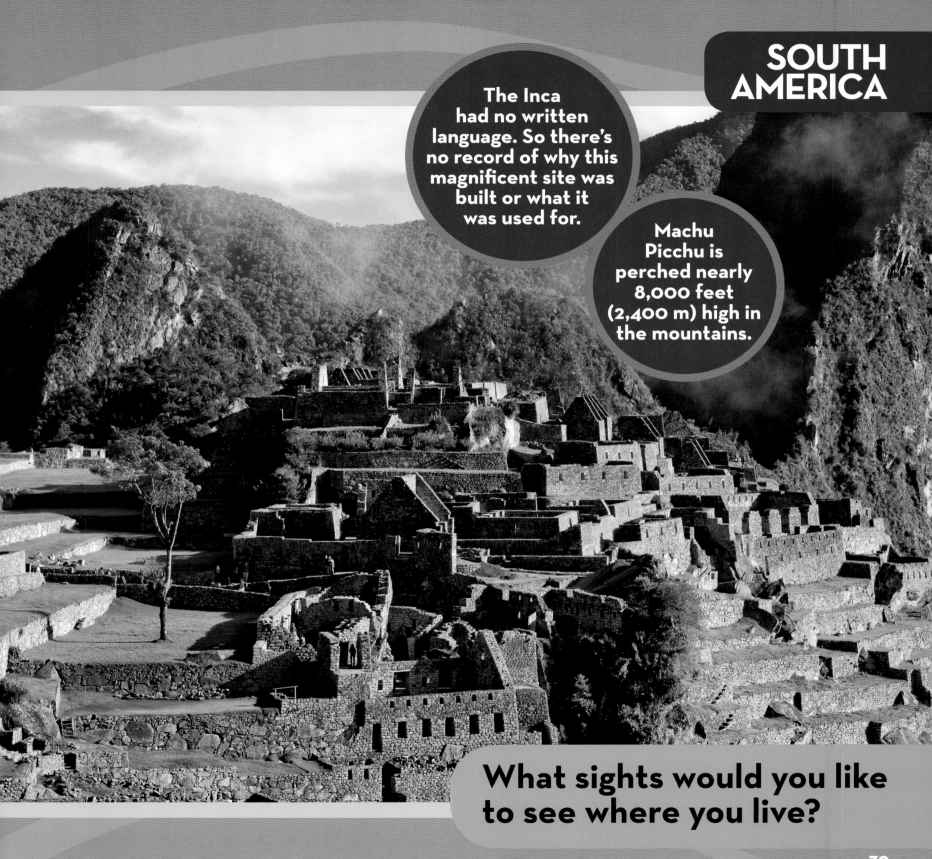

The Inca had no written language. So there's no record of why this magnificent site was built or what it was used for.

Machu Picchu is perched nearly 8,000 feet (2,400 m) high in the mountains.

What sights would you like to see where you live?

LET'S GO!

Make a rain forest

You'll need:

- a clean 2-liter soda bottle
- scissors
- tape
- small stones or pebbles
- potting soil
- plants that like moisture (moss, spider plants, or miniature ferns work well)
- water
- decorative rocks, animal figures, bits of bark (optional)

1 Ask an adult to cut off the top part of the bottle. Save the top. Use tape to cover the sharp edge.

2 Sprinkle a thin layer of pebbles over the bottom of the bottle.

3 Fill the bottle a little more than halfway with soil. Make a small hole in the soil for the plants.

4 Place the plants in the hole. Fill around them with soil.

5

To make your rain forest look more realistic, add some pebbles, rocks, animal figures, or bits of bark.

6

Water the plants by dampening the soil. Don't overwater.

7

Tape the top back onto the bottle, leaving the cap off. Place the rain forest in a bottle in a sunny spot.

CHAPTER 3
EUROPE

THE CITY OF LONDON, ENGLAND

Where old meets new

THE COUNTRIES
Countries of all sizes

Europe is the second smallest continent. But it has lots of countries. Many of the major cities are on the coasts or along Europe's long rivers.

Russia's lands stretch from Europe into Asia. Since Russia's major cities are in Europe, it's counted as a European country.

ST. BASIL'S CATHEDRAL, MOSCOW, RUSSIA

Reykjavík
ICELAND

Faroe Islands
(Denmark)

Edinburgh
UNITED
IRELAND
Dublin
KINGDOM

London

ATLANTIC OCEAN

English Channel

FRA

Bordeaux

PORTUGAL

Lisbon

ANDORRA

Madrid

SPAIN

Seville

Balearic Islands
(Spain)

GIBRALTAR
(U.K.)

A F R I

0   600 miles
0   900 kilometers

EUROPE

Barents Sea

Norwegian Sea

The name Europe comes from Europa, a princess in Greek mythology.

Shetland Islands

Orkney Islands

N O R W A Y

Oslo ⊛

S W E D E N

Stockholm ⊛

F I N L A N D

Helsinki ⊛

• St. Petersburg

⊛ Tallinn

ESTONIA

Baltic Sea

LATVIA
Riga ⊛

R U S S I A

⊛ Moscow

EUROPE-ASIA BOUNDARY

North Sea

DENMARK
Copenhagen ⊛

LITHUANIA
⊛ Vilnius

KALININGRAD
(Russia)

⊛ Minsk

B E L A R U S

Volga River

KAZAKHSTAN

NETHERLANDS
⊛ Amsterdam

• Hamburg

Berlin ⊛

Warsaw ⊛

P O L A N D

Brussels
BELGIUM

Rhine River

G E R M A N Y

• Kraków

⊛ Kiev

Volgograd •

Paris ⊛

Prague ⊛

CZECH REPUBLIC

U K R A I N E

LUXEMBOURG

Danube River

SLOVAKIA

MOLDOVA

NCE

Bern ⊛

SWITZERLAND

Vienna ⊛ ⊛ Bratislava
Budapest ⊛

Chişinău ⊛

Caspian Sea

LIECHTENSTEIN

AUSTRIA

HUNGARY

SLOVENIA

ROMANIA

Rhône R.

Ljubljana ⊛ ⊛ Zagreb

CROATIA

CRIMEA

GEORGIA
Tbilisi ⊛

Baku ⊛

SAN MARINO

BOSNIA AND HERZEGOVINA

⊛ Belgrade

Danube River

⊛ Bucharest

Black Sea

AZERBAIJAN

Sarajevo ⊛

SERBIA

ITALY

MONTENEGRO

KOSOVO
⊛ Pristina

BULGARIA

NAXCIVAN
(Azerbaijan)

Corsica (France)

VATICAN CITY

Podgorica ⊛

Sofia ⊛

⊛ Skopje

MONACO

⊛ Rome

Tirana ⊛

MACEDONIA

Naples •

ALBANIA

G R E E C E

Istanbul •

⊛ Ankara

A S I A

Sardinia (Italy)

T U R K E Y

Sicily

⊛ Athens

M e d i t e r r a n e a n   S e a

• Valletta

MALTA

Crete

NORTHERN CYPRUS

CYPRUS

⊛ Nicosia

Map Key

⊛ Country capital

• City

·········· Boundary

Disputed territory shown in light gray

45

THE **LAND**

Long rivers and curvy coastlines

Iceland

ATLANTIC
OCEAN

Europe has a lot of coastline. It wraps around many different types of bodies of water.

There are bays, seas, and gulfs. Long rivers crisscross the continent. People have used these waterways to trade goods for thousands of years.

FACTS

SIZE
3,841,000 square miles
(9,947,000 sq km)

HIGHEST MOUNTAIN
El'brus, Russia

LOWEST PLACE
Caspian Sea

LONGEST RIVER
Volga River, Russia

LARGEST LAKE
Lake Ladoga, Russia

Ireland

Great Britain

PYRENEES

IBERIAN PENINSULA

M e d

Can you spot Europe's four major rivers? They're the Rhine, the Danube, the Rhône, and the Volga.

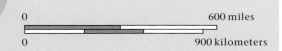

| 0 | | 600 miles |
| 0 | | 900 kilometers |

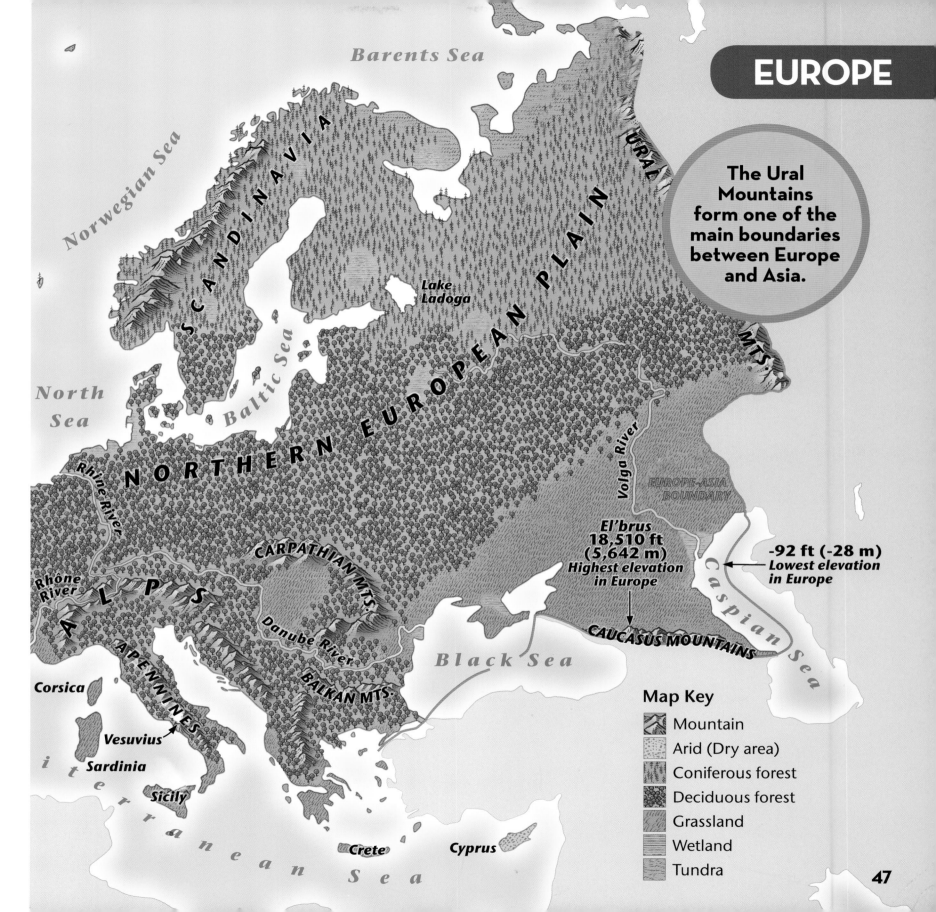

EUROPE

The Ural Mountains form one of the main boundaries between Europe and Asia.

Barents Sea

Norwegian Sea

SCANDINAVIA

URAL

MTS.

Lake
Ladoga

North
Sea

Baltic Sea

NORTHERN EUROPEAN PLAIN

Volga River

EUROPE-ASIA
BOUNDARY

Rhine River

El'brus
18,510 ft
(5,642 m)
Highest elevation
in Europe

-92 ft (-28 m)
Lowest elevation
in Europe

CARPATHIAN MTS.

Rhône
River

A L P S

Danube River

CAUCASUS MOUNTAINS

Caspian Sea

BALKAN MTS.

Black Sea

APENNINES

Corsica

Vesuvius

Sardinia

Sicily

Crete

Cyprus

Mediterranean Sea

Map Key

- Mountain
- Arid (Dry area)
- Coniferous forest
- Deciduous forest
- Grassland
- Wetland
- Tundra

BLACK FOREST
IN GERMANY

A BEACH ON THE GREEK
ISLAND OF CRETE

48

THE WEATHER

Mostly mild with plenty of rain

Warm winds blow over Europe from the Atlantic Ocean. This gives much of the continent mild weather. The land is good for farming and raising animals.

Near the Mediterranean Sea, it's warm and sunny all year-round. In the far north, it can get very cold during winter.

SHEEP IN ARCOS DE LA FRONTERA, SPAIN

THE PEOPLE

Many countries, many languages

There are many different groups of people living in Europe. More than 50 languages are spoken here. That's more than one per country!

AN ICELANDIC GIRL WITH HER LAMB

Europe has a long history. The land was once divided among many kingdoms and empires.

Children in Switzerland often study three languages in school—German, English, and French or Italian.

Imagine going to school in a gondola! If you could ride to school in any way, how would you do it?

GONDOLAS IN VENICE, ITALY

RED SQUIRREL

This eagle owl is one of the world's largest owl species.

Owls are expert hunters. Some can even take on larger prey such as foxes, opossums, and hares.

THE ANIMALS

Feathery owls and feisty squirrels

Many animals make their homes in the forests of Europe. Rabbits, squirrels, and owls are common.

ALPINE MARMOT

Reindeer and caribou are the same animal! They are known as reindeer in Europe and caribou in North America.

REINDEER

Otters snack on fish in the streams and lakes. In the north, you can find reindeer and arctic fox. Alpine marmots dig winter burrows in the slopes of the Alps.

THE SIGHTS

Stepping into history

People who lived long ago built many of the famous places throughout Europe. Stonehenge is a circle of arranged rocks in England. People built it more than 4,000 years ago. It may have helped them study the stars.

THE COLOSSEUM IN ROME, ITALY

Ancient Romans packed Rome's Colosseum to watch events such as gladiator fights.

STONEHENGE IN ENGLAND

Disneyland's Sleeping Beauty Castle is modeled after Neuschwanstein Castle in Germany.

Castles were once the homes of kings and other wealthy people. One small town in Italy had 72 castles at one time!

55

EXPLORER SPOTLIGHT

Carsten Peter visits explosive volcanoes.

Carsten Peter wears a heatproof suit. He follows scientists into the mouth of Mount Etna. It's one of the world's most active volcanoes. Mount Etna is on the island of Sicily in Italy.

Carsten's job is to take pictures of an eruption. He joins scientists as they study erupting volcanoes. The scientists want to gather samples of the melted rock, or lava. It's dangerous work. The temperature can climb to 2000°F (1093°C). Dangerous gases fill the air.

Why take the risks? Because no one knows when volcanoes will pop. Explosions can be deadly for the people living near a volcano's slopes. Information from these studies can help save lives.

LET'S GO!

Be an artist like Michelangelo

Michelangelo was a famous European artist. He painted the ceiling of the Sistine Chapel in Vatican City 500 years ago. The paintings are some of the most famous European artworks. Create your own masterpiece the way Michelangelo did! Ask for an adult's help and permission first.

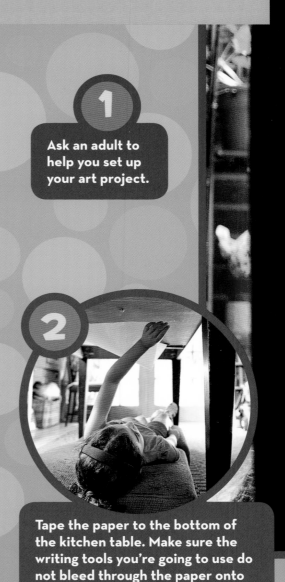

1 Ask an adult to help you set up your art project.

2 Tape the paper to the bottom of the kitchen table. Make sure the writing tools you're going to use do not bleed through the paper onto the table.

You'll need:

large sheet(s) of paper

tape

crayons, colored pencils, or washable markers

kitchen table or card table

3

Pretend you're painting the ceiling like Michelangelo. Draw your own scene on the paper.

4

Take down the paper and admire your masterpiece.

CHAPTER 4
ASIA

THE TAJ MAHAL IN AGRA, INDIA

The world's largest continent

THE COUNTRIES

Lots of land, lots of people

Everything seems bigger in Asia. More people live here than anywhere else on Earth. You'll find the most crowded cities here. Shanghai in China is home to 24 million people.

The city of Tokyo in Japan has the world's busiest metro train system.

FACTS

COUNTRIES
46

LARGEST COUNTRY
China

SMALLEST COUNTRY
Maldives

CITY WITH THE MOST PEOPLE
Tokyo, Japan. 38 million people live there.

EUROPE

Black Sea

Istanbul
Ankara ⊗ Sea
TURKEY

Mediterranean Sea
LEBANON
Beirut ⊗ SYRIA
Jerusalem ⊗⊗ Damascus
ISRAEL ⊗⊗ Amman
JORDAN

Baghdad ⊗
IRAQ
KUWAIT
Kuwait City ⊗
SAUDI
BAHRAIN
Riyadh ⊗ QATAR ⊗
Doha
ARABIA

Sanaa ⊗
YEMEN

A F R I C A

A FISHER IN SHANGHAI, CHINA

Most of Turkey is located in Asia, but the northwest part of the country lies in Europe.

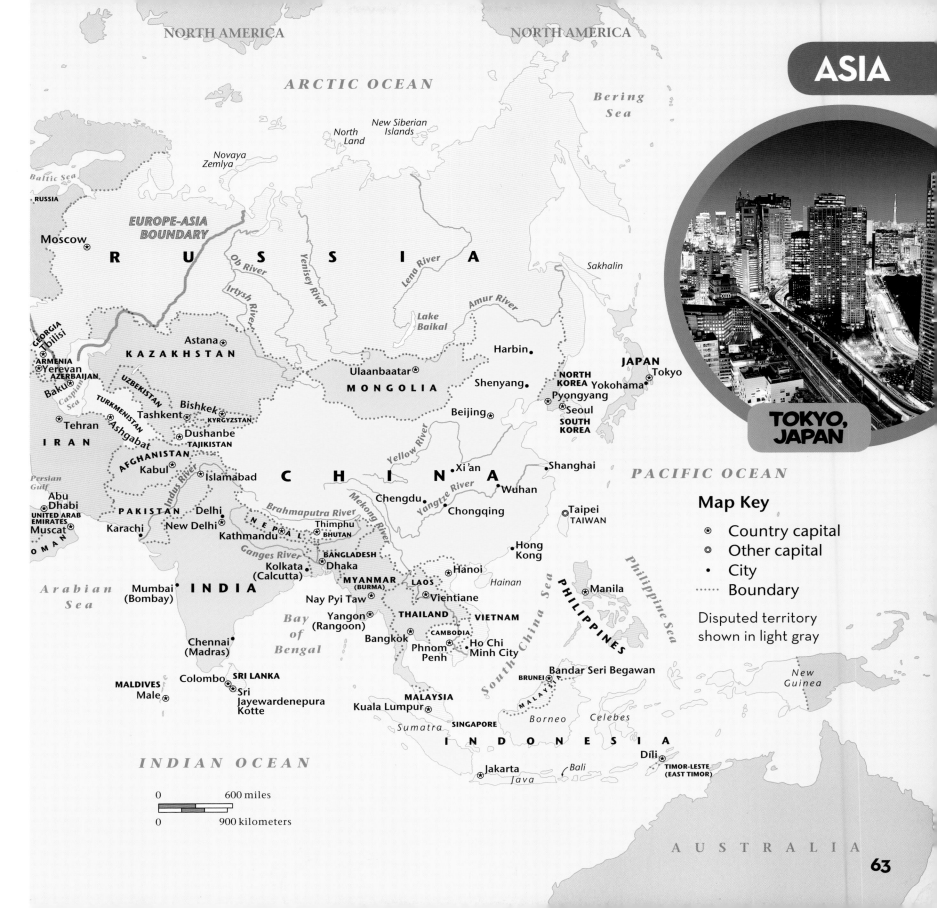

ASIA

NORTH AMERICA   **NORTH AMERICA**

ARCTIC OCEAN

Bering Sea

North Land

New Siberian Islands

Novaya Zemlya

Baltic Sea

RUSSIA

Moscow ⊛

EUROPE-ASIA BOUNDARY

R U S S I A

Ob River

Yenisey River

Irtysh River

Lena River

Amur River

Lake Baikal

Sakhalin

GEORGIA
Tbilisi ⊛

Astana ⊛

K A Z A K H S T A N

Harbin •

JAPAN

NORTH KOREA

Tokyo ⊛

ARMENIA
Yerevan ⊛
AZERBAIJAN

Baku •

Caspian Sea

UZBEKISTAN

Bishkek ⊛

Ulaanbaatar ⊛

M O N G O L I A

Shenyang •

Pyongyang ⊚

Yokohama •

TURKMENISTAN

Tashkent ⊛

KYRGYZSTAN

Beijing ⊛

Seoul ⊛
SOUTH KOREA

Tehran •

Ashgabat ⊛

Dushanbe ⊛
TAJIKISTAN

I R A N

AFGHANISTAN

Kabul ⊛

Yellow River

Xi'an •

Shanghai •

PACIFIC OCEAN

Persian Gulf

Abu Dhabi ⊚

UNITED ARAB EMIRATES

Islamabad ⊛

C H I N A

Chengdu •

Yangtze River

Wuhan •

Chongqing •

Muscat ⊛

PAKISTAN

Delhi •

Indus River

N E P A L

Brahmaputra River

Thimphu ⊛
BHUTAN

Mekong River

Taipei ⊚
TAIWAN

Hong Kong •

O M A N

Karachi •

New Delhi ⊛

Kathmandu ⊛

Hanoi ⊛

Hainan

Map Key

⊛ Country capital

⊚ Other capital

Arabian Sea

Mumbai (Bombay) •

I N D I A

Ganges River

Kolkata (Calcutta) •

BANGLADESH
Dhaka •

MYANMAR (BURMA)

LAOS

Vientiane ⊚

Manila ⊛

PHILIPPINES

Philippine Sea

• City

······ Boundary

Nay Pyi Taw ⊛

THAILAND

VIETNAM

South China Sea

Disputed territory shown in light gray

Chennai (Madras) •

Bay of Bengal

Yangon (Rangoon) ⊛

Bangkok ⊛

CAMBODIA

Ho Chi Minh City •

New Guinea

MALDIVES
Male ⊛

Colombo •
SRI LANKA

Phnom Penh ⊛

Sri Jayewardenepura Kotte ⊛

Bandar Seri Begawan ⊚

BRUNEI

M A L A Y S I A

Borneo

Celebes

Kuala Lumpur ⊛

MALAYSIA

SINGAPORE

Sumatra

I N D O N E S I A

Díli ⊚
TIMOR-LESTE (EAST TIMOR)

INDIAN OCEAN

Jakarta ⊛

Java

Bali

0   600 miles

0   900 kilometers

TOKYO, JAPAN

A U S T R A L I A

63

THE **LAND**
Rooftop of the world

You'll find ten of the world's tallest mountain peaks in Asia. They're all in one large mountain chain called the Himalaya.

Rain forests and green valleys appear south of these mountains. The land is frozen for most of the year in the north. Thirsty deserts make up most of central Asia.

MOUNT EVEREST, CHINA-NEPAL BORDER

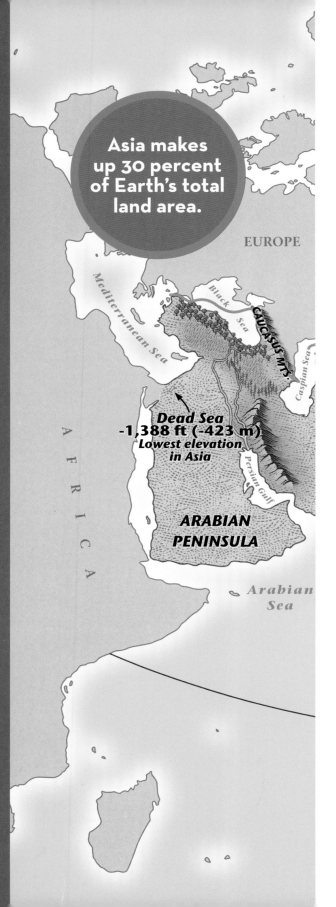

Asia makes up 30 percent of Earth's total land area.

EUROPE

Mediterranean Sea

Black Sea

CAUCASUS MTS.

Caspian Sea

Dead Sea -1,388 ft (-423 m) *Lowest elevation in Asia*

Persian Gulf

ARABIAN PENINSULA

A F R I C A

Arabian Sea

Greenland

NORTH AMERICA

NORTH AMERICA

Alaska

ARCTIC OCEAN

Bering Sea

FACTS

SIZE
17,208,000 square miles
(44,570,000 sq km)

HIGHEST MOUNTAIN
Mount Everest, China-Nepal border

LOWEST PLACE
Dead Sea, Israel-Jordan

LONGEST RIVER
Yangtze River, China

LARGEST LAKE
Lake Baikal, Russia

EUROPE-ASIA BOUNDARY

URAL MOUNTAINS

Ob River

Yenisey River

Irtysh River

Lena River

Amur River

THE STEPPES

Aral Sea

Lake Baikal

Sea of Japan (East Sea)

PACIFIC OCEAN

TIAN SHAN

GOBI

Yellow River

Brahmaputra River

HIMALAYA

Indus River

Ganges River

Mount Everest
**29,035 ft
(8,850 m)**
Highest elevation in Asia

Yangtze River

Mekong River

Bay of Bengal

South China Sea

Map Key

⛰ Mountain

Arid (Dry area)

🌲 Coniferous forest

Deciduous forest

Rain forest

Grassland

Wetland

Tundra

0	600 miles

0	900 kilometers

EQUATOR

New Guinea

Borneo

Sumatra

INDIAN OCEAN

AUSTRALIA

RIDING THROUGH
THE RAIN IN VIETNAM

THE GOBI
IN MONGOLIA
DURING WINTER

A TEA PLANTATION
IN MALAYSIA

THE WEATHER

Very cold or hot; very rainy or very dry

Northern Asia has long, icy winters and short, cool summers. It rarely rains in the deserts in Asia's central and western parts.

In the south, heavy rains soak the land in the summer. The rains allow farmers to grow water-loving crops like rice.

Most of the world's rice is grown in Asia.

A RICE PADDY

67

THE PEOPLE

Land of many traditions

KIDS AT SCHOOL IN THAILAND

Many different groups of people live in Asia. They each have their own language and culture. Some traditions are very old.

The world's first cities were built here thousands of years ago.

WAITING FOR A BUS IN INDIA

Millions of people visit Mecca, Saudi Arabia, every year for a religious journey. The tradition is part of the Muslim faith and is called a hajj. It's the world's largest gathering.

A PILGRIMAGE AT MECCA IN SAUDI ARABIA

What are your family's favorite traditions?

A Bengal tiger's roar can be heard up to two miles (3 km) away.

Fuzzy pandas live only in the bamboo forests of China.

THE
ANIMALS

Lizards, tigers, and bears!

Tigers prowl the forests of India and some other parts of Asia. The world's largest lizard lives in Asia. It's called the Komodo dragon.

KOMODO DRAGON

YAK

Woolly yaks live high up in the Himalaya.

71

THE SIGHTS

Ancient temples, super skyscrapers, and a great wall

Temples and the ruins of old cities can be found throughout Asia. Angkor Wat in Cambodia is a huge temple that was built over 900 years ago.

THE GREAT WALL OF CHINA

China's Great Wall is the largest structure built by humans. It was built in sections over hundreds of years. The wall is 13,000 miles (20,921 km) long!

Angkor Wat in Cambodia was originally a Hindu temple. Its name means "city of temples."

THE BURJ KHALIFA BUILDING

Burj Khalifa in the United Arab Emirates is a new marvel. It's the world's tallest skyscraper. It's as tall as nine Statues of Liberty stacked on top of each other.

73

LET'S GO!

Design a mosaic

Some sites in Asia are famous for their mosaics. These beautiful, patterned tiles decorate places like the Blue Mosque in Turkey and the Taj Mahal in India. You can make your own mosaic!

You'll need:

pencil

ruler

scissors

colored construction paper cut into a variety of shapes, such as triangles, diamonds, pentagons, squares (Draw the shapes on the paper first. Make sure that each shape is the same size and that you have enough of each to make a repeating pattern.)

3 or more pieces of cardboard

glue

1 Arrange the pattern blocks or shapes on one cardboard square. Once you're happy with the design, glue the shapes to the square. This is one "tile."

2 You can make as many tiles as you like.

3 Put the tiles together. Count how many different shapes you used in your mosaic. Which shape did you use the most?

75

CHAPTER 5
AFRICA

Life on the move

THE COUNTRIES

The most of any continent

Of all the continents, Africa is divided into the most countries.

The newest country is South Sudan. It was created in 2011.

Africa has 18,500 miles (30,000 km) of coastline.

A boy carries a tray of fresh bread through busy streets in Cairo, Egypt.

Some cities are very crowded. But most Africans live in smaller villages and farms.

Canary Islands (Spain)

WESTERN SAHARA (Morocco)

Nouakchott
MA
CABO VERDE
Praia
Dakar
SENEGAL
Banjul
GAMBIA
Bissau
GUINEA-BISSAU
Conakry
GUI
Freetown
SIERRA LEONE

FACTS

COUNTRIES
54

LARGEST COUNTRY
Algeria

SMALLEST COUNTRY
Seychelles

CITY WITH THE MOST PEOPLE
Cairo, Egypt. 18 million people live there.

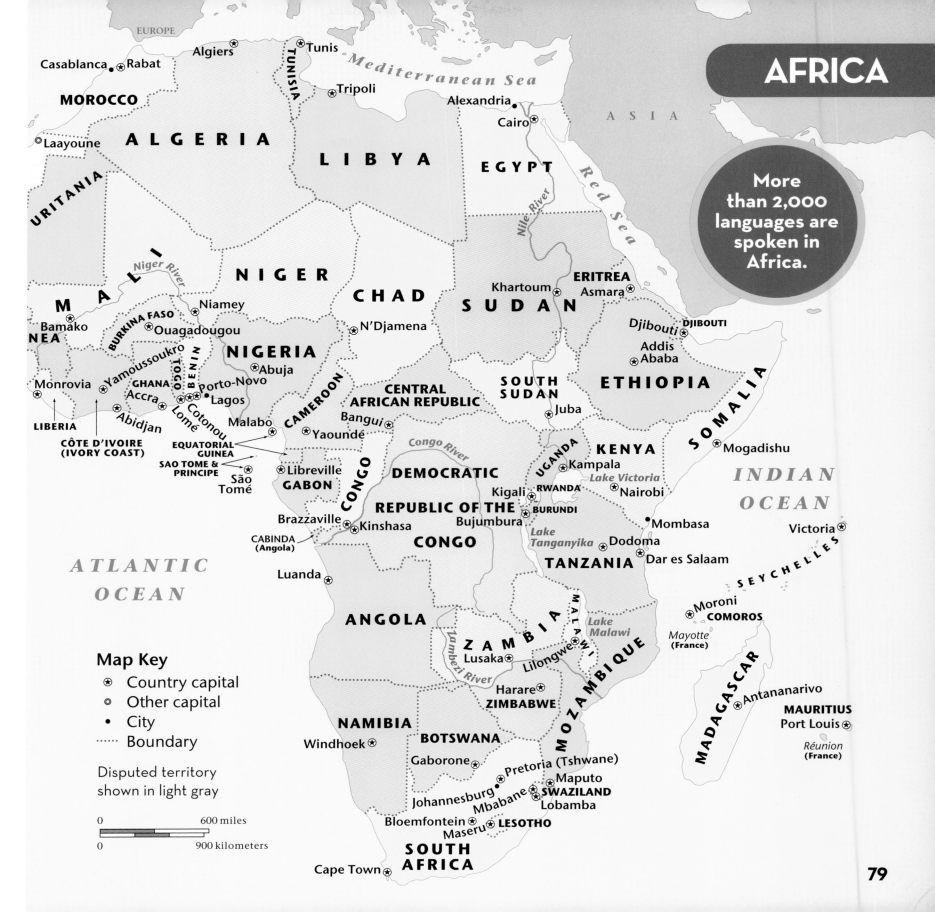

AFRICA

More than 2,000 languages are spoken in Africa.

EUROPE

Casablanca • ⊛Rabat Algiers⊛ Tunis⊛
MOROCCO TUNISIA ⊛Tripoli
⊙Laayoune **A L G E R I A** **L I B Y A** Alexandria •
Cairo⊛ A S I A

Mediterranean Sea

URITANIA *Nile River* Red Sea

M A L I *Niger River* **N I G E R** **C H A D** Khartoum⊛ **ERITREA**
Bamako⊛ Niamey⊛ **S U D A N** Asmara⊛
NEA **BURKINA FASO** N'Djamena• Djibouti⊛ **DJIBOUTI**
⊛Ouagadougou Addis
NIGERIA Ababa⊛
Yamoussoukro⊛ ⊛Abuja **SOUTH** **ETHIOPIA**
Monrovia⊛ **GHANA** Porto-Novo⊛ **SUDAN**
Accra⊛ Lagos• **CENTRAL** Juba⊛
LIBERIA Abidjan⊛ Cotonou• **AFRICAN REPUBLIC** **SOMALIA**
CÔTE D'IVOIRE Lomé Malabo⊛ **CAMEROON** Bangui⊛
(IVORY COAST) ⊛Yaoundé **KENYA** ⊛Mogadishu
SAO TOME & Kampala⊛
PRINCIPE São ⊛Libreville **DEMOCRATIC** **UGANDA** *Lake Victoria*
Tomé **GABON** *Congo River* Kigali⊛ **RWANDA** ⊛Nairobi
REPUBLIC OF THE ⊛ **BURUNDI**
Brazzaville⊛ Bujumbura Mombasa•
CABINDA ⊛Kinshasa *Lake* **INDIAN**
(Angola) **CONGO** *Tanganyika* Dodoma⊛ **OCEAN**
Luanda⊛ Dar es Salaam•
TANZANIA **SEYCHELLES**
Victoria⊛

ATLANTIC
OCEAN **A N G O L A** **MALAWI** *Lake* Moroni⊛
Malawi **COMOROS** *Mayotte*
Z A M B I A *(France)*
Zambezi River Lusaka⊛ Lilongwe⊛
Harare⊛ Antananarivo⊛
ZIMBABWE **MADAGASCAR** **MAURITIUS**
Port Louis⊛

Map Key
⊛ Country capital
⊙ Other capital
• City
⋯⋯ Boundary

Disputed territory
shown in light gray

NAMIBIA **MOZAMBIQUE** *Réunion*
Windhoek⊛ **BOTSWANA** *(France)*
Gaborone⊛ Pretoria (Tshwane)⊛ Maputo•
Johannesburg• Mbabane⊛ **SWAZILAND**
Bloemfontein⊛ Maseru⊛ **LESOTHO** Lobamba

0 ___ 600 miles
0 ___ 900 kilometers

SOUTH
Cape Town⊛ **AFRICA**

THE **LAND**

Dry deserts in the north and south, lush forests in the middle

Most of Africa is on a high, flat plateau. There aren't many mountains here. Most craggy peaks are in the east.

You'll find deserts at the northern and southern parts of Africa. A band of forests and grasslands called savannas make up the middle.

ZEBRAS IN TANZANIA

FACTS

SIZE
11,608,000 square miles
(30,065,000 sq km)

HIGHEST MOUNTAIN
Kilimanjaro, Tanzania

LOWEST PLACE
Lake Assal, Djibouti

LONGEST RIVER
Nile River

LARGEST LAKE
Lake Victoria

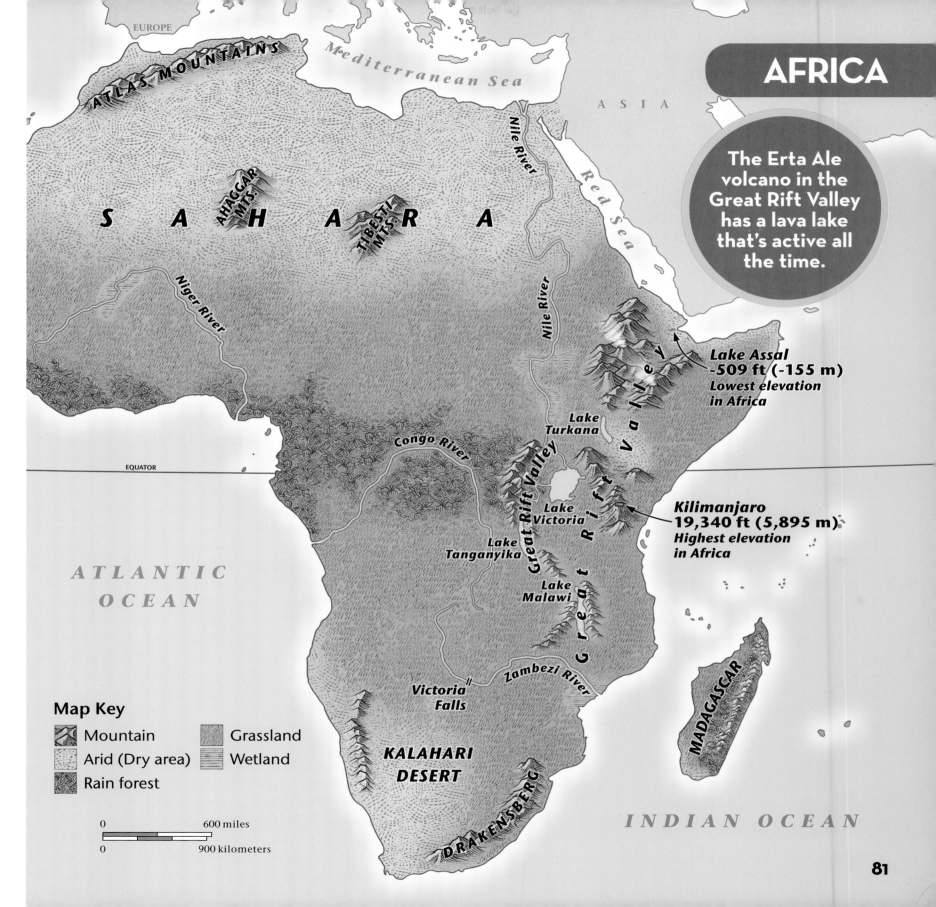

EUROPE

Mediterranean Sea

ASIA

ATLAS MOUNTAINS

Nile River

Red Sea

AFRICA

The Erta Ale volcano in the Great Rift Valley has a lava lake that's active all the time.

S A H A R A

AHAGGAR MTS.

TIBESTI MTS.

Niger River

Nile River

Congo River

EQUATOR

Lake Turkana

Great Rift Valley

Lake Assal
-509 ft (-155 m)
Lowest elevation in Africa

Lake Victoria

Lake Tanganyika

Kilimanjaro
19,340 ft (5,895 m)
Highest elevation in Africa

ATLANTIC OCEAN

Lake Malawi

Great Rift Valley

Zambezi River

Victoria Falls

MADAGASCAR

Map Key

Mountain

Arid (Dry area)

Rain forest

Grassland

Wetland

KALAHARI DESERT

DRAKENSBERG

INDIAN OCEAN

0   600 miles

0   900 kilometers

A RAIN FOREST
IN UGANDA

KILIMANJARO, TANZANIA

THE WEATHER

Dry, hot, and rainy

Most places in Africa are very hot. The continent doesn't have any cold–weather environments. It's rainy in the middle of Africa. You'll find rain forests there. North Africa contains the world's largest hot desert—the Sahara.

CAMEL CARAVAN IN THE SAHARA

Strong winds in the Sahara can cause sand storms.

How would you stay cool in the desert?

THE PEOPLE

Our ancient origins

NAIROBI, KENYA

People have lived in Africa longer than any other place. Scientists think that humans came from here.

STUDENTS IN SWAZILAND

Today, many groups of people live in Africa. Some focus on farming and herding. Others live in booming cities where there are lots of businesses.

Masai houses are usually circular or star-shaped.

MASAI CHILDREN IN FRONT OF A MUD HUT, MASAI MARA, KENYA

The giraffe is Earth's tallest animal.

HIPPOPOTAMUS

THE ANIMALS

Time for a safari!

Africa is famous for its animal life. You'll find herds of elephants, prides of lions, and towers of giraffes.

A MOTHER LION AND HER CUBS

GORILLA

In the forests of central Africa, gorillas munch peacefully on leaves.

Hungry hippos wade through the rivers and lakes.

THE SIGHTS

Pyramids, wildlife, and waterfalls

Visitors are awed by Egypt's Great Sphinx and pyramids. The ancient Egyptians built them 4,500 years ago.

Every zebra has its own unique stripe pattern.

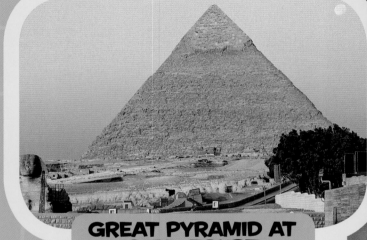

GREAT PYRAMID AT GIZA, EGYPT

Animal lovers go to the grasslands to see Africa's great animal herds.

VICTORIA FALLS,
ZAMBEZI RIVER, ZIMBABWE

Victoria Falls is one of Africa's natural wonders.
Its African name means "smoke that thunders."
The falls create mist that can be spotted from
more than 12 miles (19 km) away.

EXPLORER SPOTLIGHT

Jane Goodall uncovers the world of chimpanzees.

In 1960, Jane Goodall traveled to Africa, packing a pair of binoculars and a notebook. She wanted to learn everything she could about chimpanzees. These apes are humans' closest animal relatives.

Jane lived near chimps in the forests and went to watch them every day. She observed their behavior and took notes. She made many new discoveries. Her work turned into one of the longest studies of chimpanzee behavior.

The descendants of the chimps Jane studied in the 1960s still live in Gombe National Park.

LET'S GO!

Watch animals like a scientist

Jane Goodall made important discoveries about animals by simply watching them. Make a field guide of animal life in your neighborhood.

1 Take your supplies into your backyard or on a walk through your neighborhood. (Get an adult's permission first.)

2 Note the animals you see. What are they doing? What are they eating? Note if animals interact with each other. You can use your colored pencils to draw pictures of them, too.

You'll need:

notebook

pen or pencil

colored pencils (optional)

binoculars (optional)

3 Try to do your observations at the same time each day, or once a week. Write down any changes that take place.

4 After a few weeks or months, go back and look at your notes. Do you notice any changes happening over time?

5 Continue your observations for as long as you like!

93

CHAPTER 6
AUSTRALIA

A RING-TAILED DRAGON LIZARD
IN SHARK BAY, AUSTRALIA

The land down under

THE COUNTRIES

Australia is a country and a continent in one.

Australia is the smallest of the seven continents. It makes up just 5 percent of Earth's land.

BLUE-WINGED KOOKABURRA

It is the only continent that is also a country. It is made up of six states. Australia is called "the land down under" because the whole country is south of, or "under," the Equator.

FACTS

COUNTRIES
1

STATE WITH THE MOST PEOPLE
New South Wales

STATE WITH THE FEWEST PEOPLE
Tasmania

CITY WITH THE MOST PEOPLE
Sydney. 4.5 million people live there.

WE
AUS

Perth

INDIAN
OCEAN

• Darwin

Gulf of Carpentaria

NORTHERN TERRITORY

Cairns •

Townsville •

• Mount Isa

Mackay •

QUEENSLAND

Alice • Springs

A U S T R A L I A

• Rockhampton

Australia may be the smallest continent, but it is the sixth largest country on Earth.

STERN TRALIA

SOUTH AUSTRALIA

Lake Eyre

Brisbane ◉

◉ Gold Coast

Darling River

NEW SOUTH WALES

PACIFIC OCEAN

GREAT AUSTRALIAN BIGHT

Adelaide ◉

KANGAROO ISLAND

Murray River

◉ Sydney

Canberra ⊛

JERVIS BAY TERRITORY

AUSTRALIAN CAPITAL TERRITORY

VICTORIA

Map Key
⊛ Country capital
◉ State or territory capital
• City
⋯⋯ Boundary
▨ Dry salt lake

Melbourne ◉

| 0 | | 600 miles |
| 0 | | 900 kilometers |

TASMANIA

◉ Hobart

THE LAND

A dry and flat outback and thousands of islands

A mountain range runs down Australia's east coast. It blocks rain from the Pacific Ocean. The rest of the continent is dry and flat. The interior is nicknamed the outback.

Eucalyptus and acacia trees are the most common plants found in Australia. Tasmania has large areas of rain forests and mountains.

ULURU

Uluru (also known as Ayers Rock) is a huge sandstone rock in the Australian outback. It stands taller than the Eiffel Tower in Paris, France.

INDIAN OCEAN

Hamersley Range

Darling Range

FACTS

SIZE
2,989,000 square miles
(7,741,000 sq km)

HIGHEST MOUNTAIN
Mount Kosciuszko

LOWEST PLACE
Lake Eyre

LONGEST RIVER
Darling River

LARGEST LAKE
Lake Eyre, but it's rarely full of water and is dry for part of the year.

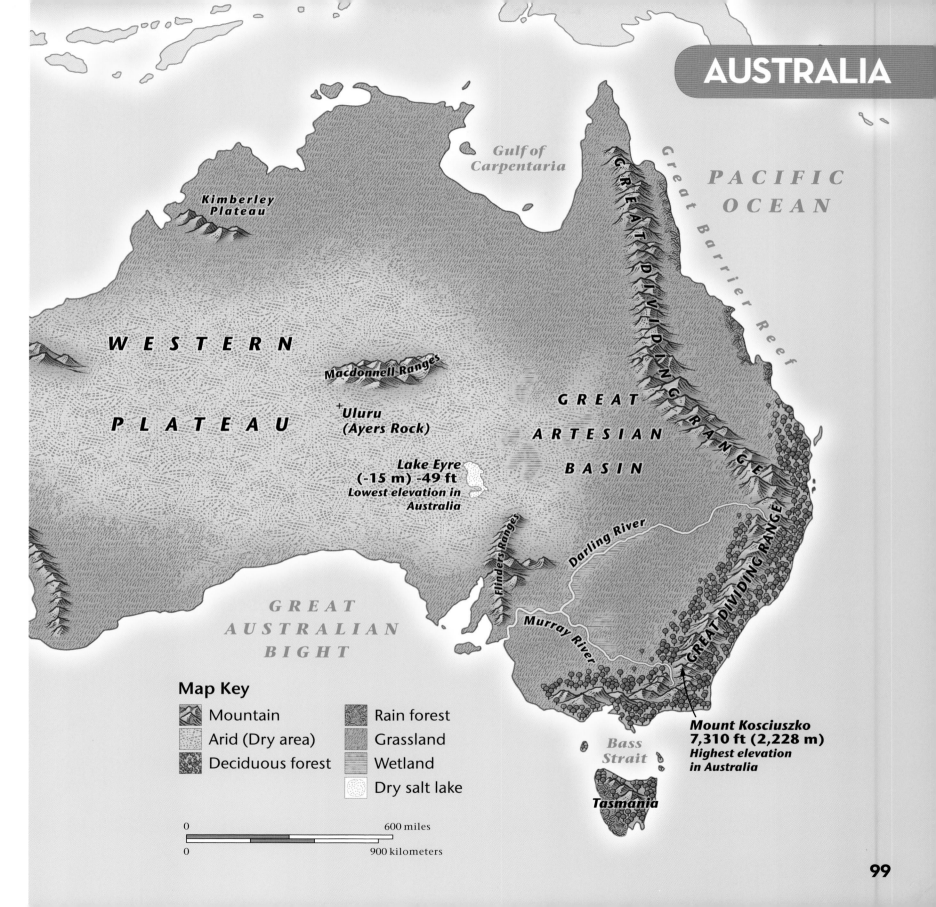

AUSTRALIA

Kimberley Plateau

Gulf of Carpentaria

PACIFIC OCEAN

Great Barrier Reef

WESTERN PLATEAU

Macdonnell Ranges

GREAT DIVIDING RANGE

+Uluru (Ayers Rock)

GREAT ARTESIAN BASIN

Lake Eyre
(-15 m) -49 ft
Lowest elevation in Australia

Flinders Ranges

Darling River

Murray River

GREAT DIVIDING RANGE

GREAT AUSTRALIAN BIGHT

Map Key

Mountain

Arid (Dry area)

Deciduous forest

Rain forest

Grassland

Wetland

Dry salt lake

Mount Kosciuszko
7,310 ft (2,228 m)
Highest elevation in Australia

Bass Strait

Tasmania

0   600 miles

0   900 kilometers

LIMESTONE ROCK TOWERS IN THE AUSTRALIAN DESERT

MILLAA MILLAA FALLS IN QUEENSLAND, AUSTRALIA

THE WEATHER

Sunscreen is a must!

Most of Australia is warm and sunny all the time. Ocean winds bring rain to the coasts. This causes thick forests to grow in some areas.

Hurricanes are a summer weather threat in the region. In this part of the world, hurricanes have a different name. They are called cyclones.

A STORM OVER SYDNEY HARBOR

THE PEOPLE

Ocean crossers on the move

Aboriginals first came to Australia from Asia about 40,000 years ago. They have one of the world's oldest cultures. Storytelling, painting, and dance are all important parts of their lives.

Today, most Australians are related to settlers from Europe who first arrived about 200 years ago. English is the main language.

ABORIGINAL GIRLS WITH FACE PAINT

A SURFING COMPETITION IN SYDNEY, AUSTRALIA

Australian cattle ranches are called stations. There are many across the country.

THE ANIMALS

Kangaroo crossing!

GREEN SEA TURTLE

KOALA

Many unusual animals live in Australia. Koalas, kangaroos, and wallabies raise their babies in pouches in their bellies. The duck-billed platypus is a mammal like us. But its babies hatch out of eggs!

PLATYPUS

Green sea turtles are found off the coast and sometimes come up on land to get some sun.

WALLABIES

CROWN-OF-THORNS SEA STAR

In the coral reefs of the Great Barrier Reef, crown-of-thorns sea stars have become a problem. They hurt the underwater environment by eating corals.

105

THE SIGHTS

Fun in the water and on land

SURFER AT SNAPPER ROCKS, GOLD COAST

The Great Barrier Reef is Earth's largest living structure. It's off Australia's northeastern coast. Australia's beautiful beaches are popular surfing spots. There's even a city named Surfers Paradise!

Would you rather learn how to surf or scuba dive?

SYDNEY OPERA HOUSE

THE GREAT BARRIER REEF

The Sydney Opera House is one of Australia's most famous places to visit. It hosts plays, dances, and concerts.

LET'S GO!

Leap like a kangaroo

Red kangaroos can cover 25 feet (7.6 m) in a single leap. How does your longest leap compare to a jumping roo's?

You'll need:

masking tape

tape measure

flat ground

marker

RED KANGAROO

1 Make a line on the ground with masking tape. This is the starting point of your jump.

2 Get a running start and jump from the line you just made. Remember to practice your jumping safely.

3 Mark your landing spot with a piece of tape. Use the tape measure to measure the distance between the starting line and your landing spot.

4 Make several jumps and mark each jump with a piece of tape.

5 Label each try, "Jump 1," "Jump 2," "Jump 3," and so on.

6 Which jump was the longest? How does it measure up to a red kangaroo's?

CHAPTER 7
ANTARCTICA

GENTOO PENGUINS ON AN ICEBERG IN THE ANTARCTIC PENINSULA

Can you feel the chill?

THE **LAND**

A frozen landscape

Antarctica is Earth's coldest, driest, and windiest place. This landmass covers the South Pole.

There are no countries. But scientists from all over the world have set up research stations here to study the land, weather, and animals.

FACTS

SIZE
5,100,000 square miles
(13,209,000 sq km)

HIGHEST MOUNTAIN
Vinson Massif

LOWEST PLACE
Byrd Glacier

Antarctica is the world's largest cold desert.

KITCHEN DINING

ANTARCTICA

AFRICA
ATLANTIC OCEAN
SOUTH AMERICA
INDIAN OCEAN
ANTARCTICA
PACIFIC OCEAN
AUSTRALIA

INDIAN OCEAN

Weddell Sea

QUEEN MAUD LAND

ENDERBY LAND

PENINSULA

RONNE ICE SHELF

Berkner Island

ELLSWORTH LAND

Sea

Vinson Massif
16,067 ft (4,897 m)
Highest elevation in Antarctica

WEST ANTARCTICA

South Pole

A N T A R C T I C A

EAST ANTARCTICA

SHACKLETON ICE SHELF

TRANSANTARCTIC MOUNTAINS

Amundsen Sea

MARIE BYRD LAND

ROSS ICE SHELF

Byrd Glacier
-9,416 ft (-2,870 m)
Lowest elevation in Antarctica

Roosevelt Island

Ross Island
Mount Erebus

Ross Sea

WILKES LAND

INDIAN OCEAN

Map Key

Mountain
Ice cap
Glacier
Ice shelf

◆ Research station

0   600 miles
0   900 kilometers

What's your favorite season?

OLYMPUS RANGE IN VICTORIA LAND, ANTARCTICA

The Olympus mountain range surrounds Antarctica's Dry Valleys.

These valleys get their name from the high winds that constantly blast away snow, leaving the land bare.

THE WEATHER

Pack your coat!

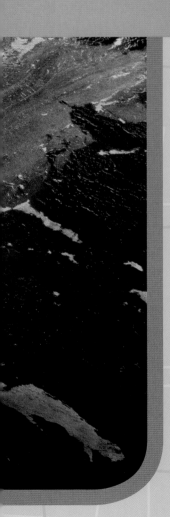

It's no surprise—it is cold in Antarctica year-round. Temperatures rarely rise above freezing. The continent gets very little rain or snow. That makes Antarctica a big cold desert.

The thick layer of ice covering the continent actually took millions of years to build up.

A BLIZZARD NEAR THE SOUTH POLE

BLUE-EYED CORMORANT

Sea birds such as penguins (above) and cormorants (left) feast on the plentiful fish that live in the waters around Antarctica.

EMPEROR PENGUINS

THE ANIMALS

It's a penguin parade.

LEOPARD SEAL

It might seem like nothing could survive in Antarctica. But that's not the case. Some animals are built for life here. Emperor penguins live on Antarctica year-round.

HUMPBACK WHALE

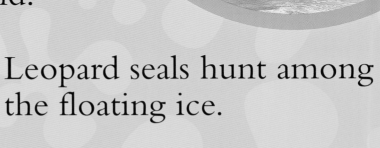

Leopard seals hunt among the floating ice.

Blue and humpback whales swim through Antarctic waters in the summer.

EXPLORER SPOTLIGHT

Roald Amundsen was the first explorer to reach the South Pole.

He planted Norway's flag at the South Pole on December 14, 1911. He and his team risked their lives to explore the frozen continent.

They had to drag supplies across 900 miles (1,500 km) of ice and back again. They wore heavy furs. For 99 days, they lived off food such as dried meat, raisins, and cocoa (what chocolate is made of).

Amundsen's success helped people learn more about polar exploration and the conditions in Antarctica.

LET'S GO!

Take care of a penguin "egg"

Mommy and daddy emperor penguins take turns caring for their egg. The penguin parent holds the egg on its feet to keep it warm. Try taking care of your own egg.

1 Place the orange on your feet. Gently support it by squeezing it with your feet. This is your penguin egg.

You'll need:

one orange

2 Now try to walk around like a penguin. Remember to waddle with your feet together, supporting your egg.

EMPEROR PENGUIN PARENTS TAKING TURNS CARING FOR THEIR EGG

EGG

121

PARENT TIPS

YOU CAN REINFORCE AN UNDERSTANDING OF PLACE, DIRECTION, AND MAP READING BEYOND THE PAGES OF THIS BOOK. The time you spend extending these concepts can pay off greatly. Geography can be an abstract concept for children. Often, our kids are magically transported from here to there—usually via the Parent Taxi Service! Involve your child in the planning of routes. Explain directionality using natural markers such as the rising and setting sun and the North Star. City kids can help determine which subway or bus lines to take using your transit system's map.

Here are some other activities you can do after reading National Geographic's *Little Kids First Big Book of the World*.

THREADS OF THE WORLD
(Search Strategy)

Many of the goods that we buy are actually produced and shipped from faraway places. Your child can build a solid understanding of this by rummaging through her closet. With your child, look at the tags on her clothes and note the country where each piece was made. Make a list and mark the locations on the world map in this book. Discuss any trends you notice with your child. Did more clothes come from any particular continent?

GEO JAMS
(Music)

Explore the origins of the music you listen to in your home. What kinds of instruments are used to make your child's favorite tunes? Where do they come from? Drums and shakers are great examples of instruments that are made differently depending on a people's culture and location. For example, Inuit musicians make drums out of wood and caribou skin. During dances, Cherokee women wear leg rattles made of tortoise shells with pebbles inside. Ask your child to draw a picture of an instrument he would create if designing one from scratch. See if you can make the instrument using regular household objects.

BLOCK PARTY
(Math)

Help your child use blocks to make a 3-D map of your neighborhood. Label the block that represents your house, the one that represents your child's school, the neighborhood playground, and so on. Younger children can trace blocks onto paper to make a 2-D map. Then, take the map with you on your next outing. Use it to navigate to your destination. Make a wrong turn? That's a great opportunity to teach your child about the importance of revising your work after you've tested it.

MAPS EVERYWHERE
(Arts and Crafts)

Displaying maps in your home is a great way to incorporate them into your routines. Maps can appear in unexpected places. (Check out shower curtain maps, map placemats, map posters, and map bulletin boards.) Hang a country or world map and insert push pins into all the places your family has visited. Or, have your child interview family members to find out where your family and their ancestors are originally from. Mark these locations on a map and include family pictures, if available. You can even create your own map puzzle. Give your child a map that you don't use and allow her to cut it into jigsaw-shaped pieces.

MAKE A MODEL
(Geography/Landforms)

Use modeling clay to form geographic features, such as islands, mountains, and valleys. If available, make models in a disposable baking dish with plasticine, a type of clay that doesn't absorb water. Pour water into the dish to model the water and land features. For younger kids, make expanding oceans. Draw the seven continents on a coffee filter. Roughly fill in the oceans in blue. Spray water on the filter and watch the blue "water" spread.

GAMES OF THE GLOBE
(Exercise)

Many popular sports originated in other places. With your child, research the roots of his favorite sport. Have the rules and equipment changed since the sport became popular here? If they have, try to organize a pick-up game of the sport that incorporates some of the original rules. For example, if your children's favorite sport is baseball, take a look at how cricket, the sport that inspired baseball, was played. How could you tweak your game to include some of the rules of cricket?

IMAGINARY ISLAND
(Creative Thinking)

Teach your child about map symbols and legends by having her create a map of an imaginary secret island. The island can be the location of anything: a pirate hideout, an alien spaceship landing site, a tropical resort for unicorns—you name it! The map must include symbols and a legend, or key, that explains what each symbol means.

VISIT ONLINE
(Technology)

For more geography education resources and map exploration tools, visit:

education.nationalgeographic.com/education

kids.nationalgeographic.com

nationalgeographic.com/
kids-world-atlas/maps.html

GLOSSARY

ATLAS
a book of maps

CARAVAN
a group of people, usually traders, traveling across a desert in Africa or Asia

CLIMATE
the average weather conditions of a place

CONTINENT
one of the world's main expanses of land

DESERT
a dry area of land that receives fewer than ten inches (25 cm) of rain or snow a year

EQUATOR
an imaginary line around the Earth that divides the planet into northern and southern hemispheres, or halves

ERUPTION
the release of lava and/or gas from a vent in a volcano

EXPLORATION
the act of traveling through an unfamiliar area to learn about it

GLACIER
a slowly moving mass of ice usually found high up in mountains or near the poles

GLADIATORS
men trained to fight with weapons against other men or animals for sport

GONDOLA
a flat-bottomed boat that is commonly used as transportation through canals in Venice, Italy

GOODS
items such as food or clothing that are commonly sold in a marketplace

LANDMASS
a large chunk of land, such as a continent or a large island

MAMMAL
a warm-blooded animal whose young feed on milk produced by the mother

MOSAIC
a picture or pattern usually made by arranging pieces of glass or tile

MOSQUE
a place of worship for people of the Muslim religion

MYTHOLOGY
a collection of stories that belong to one culture or religion

OBSERVE
to notice something and believe it's important or figure out that it's not important

PILGRIMAGE
a religious journey usually made to a sacred place

PLATEAU
an area of high ground that is flat

PREY
animals that are hunted and killed by another animal for food

PYRAMID
a large structure with a square or triangular base and sloping sides that meet in a point at the top

RAIN FOREST
a dense forest that receives more than 60 inches (152 cm) of rain a year

SETTLER
a person who moves into an undeveloped area to live there

SPECIES
a group of similar organisms that can produce young

TERRITORY
an area of land under the control of another country's government

VOLCANO
An opening in Earth's crust (usually at the top of a mountain or hill) where lava, ash, and gases from deep inside Earth escape

INDEX

PHOTO CREDITS

Staff for This Book

Priyanka Sherman, Amy Briggs, *Project Editors*

Eva Absher-Schantz, *Art Director*

Lori Epstein, *Senior Photo Editor*

Carl Mehler, *Director of Maps*

Juan José Valdés, *The Geographer*

Martha Sharma, *Geography Consultant*

Paige Towler, *Editorial Assistant*

Maureen J. Flynn, Julie A. Ibinson, Michael Fry, *Map Editors*

Michael McNey and Martin S. Walz, *Map Production*

Erica Holsclaw, *Special Projects Assistant*

Rachel Kenny, *Design Production Assistant*

Michael Cassady, *Rights Clearance Specialist*

Grace Hill, *Managing Editor*

Joan Gossett, *Senior Production Editor*

Lewis R. Bassford, *Production Manager*

George Bounelis, *Manager, Production Services*

Susan Borke, *Legal and Business Affairs*

Published by the National Geographic Society

Gary E. Knell, *President and Chief Executive Officer*

John M. Fahey, *Chairman of the Board*

Melina Gerosa Bellows, *Chief Education Officer*

Declan Moore, *Chief Media Officer*

Hector Sierra, *Senior Vice President and General Manager, Book Division*

Senior Management Team, Kids Publishing and Media

Nancy Laties Feresten, *Senior Vice President*
Jennifer Emmett, *Vice President, Editorial Director, Kids Books*
Julie Vosburgh Agnone, *Vice President, Editorial Operations*
Rachel Buchholz, *Editor and Vice President, NG Kids magazine*
Michelle Sullivan, *Vice President, Kids Digital*
Eva Absher-Schantz, *Design Director*
Jay Sumner, *Photo Director*
Hannah August, *Marketing Director*
R. Gary Colbert, *Production Director*

Digital

Anne McCormack, *Director*
Laura Goertzel, Sara Zeglin, *Producers*
Jed Winer, *Special Projects Assistant*
Emma Rigney, *Creative Producer*
Brian Ford, *Video Producer*
Bianca Bowman, *Assistant Producer*
Natalie Jones, *Senior Product Manager*

The National Geographic Society is one of the world's largest nonprofit scientific and educational organizations. Founded in 1888 to "increase and diffuse geographic knowledge," the Society's mission is to inspire people to care about the planet. It reaches more than 400 million people worldwide each month through its official journal, *National Geographic*, and other magazines; National Geographic Channel; television documentaries; music; radio; films; books; DVDs; maps; exhibitions; live events; school publishing programs; interactive media; and merchandise. National Geographic has funded more than 10,000 scientific research, conservation, and exploration projects and supports an education program promoting geographic literacy.

For more information, please visit nationalgeographic .com, call 1-800-NGS LINE (647-5463), or write to the following address:
National Geographic Society
1145 17th Street N.W.
Washington, D.C. 20036-4688 U.S.A.

Visit us online at nationalgeographic.com/books

For librarians and teachers: ngchildrensbooks.org

More for kids from National Geographic:
kids.nationalgeographic.com

For information about special discounts for bulk purchases, please contact National Geographic Books Special Sales: ngspecsales@ngs.org

For rights or permissions inquiries, please contact National Geographic Books Subsidiary Rights: ngbookrights@ngs.org

Hardcover ISBN: 978-1-4263-2050-7
Reinforced Library Edition ISBN: 978-1-4263-2051-4

Printed in Hong Kong
15/THK/1